KIDS ON EARTH

Wildlife Adventures – Explore The World
Sumatran Tiger - Indonesia

Sensei Paul David

COPYRIGHT PAGE

Kids On Earth: Wildlife Adventures - Explore The World

Sumatran Tiger - Indonesia

by Sensei Paul David,

Copyright © 2023.

All rights reserved.

978-1-77848-205-2 KoE_WildLife_Amazon_PaperbackBook_indonesia_sumatran tiger

978-1-77848-204-5 KoE_WildLife_Amazon_eBook_indonesia_sumatran tiger

978-1-77848-432-2 KoE_Wildlife_Ingram_PaperbackBook_SumatranTiger

This book is not authorized for free distribution copying.

www.senseipublishing.com

@senseipublishing
#senseipublishing

Synopsis

This book is a non-fiction children's book for ages 6 to 12 about the Sumatran Tiger in Indonesia. It provides 30 fun and unique facts about the Sumatran Tiger that you won't find anywhere else. From the tiger's looks and behavior, to its habitat and diet, this book has taught you all about this incredible species and its place in the Indonesian rainforest. It includes an introduction, 30 fun facts about the Sumatran Tiger, and a conclusion. It also provides an overview of the threats to the species and encourages readers to help protect the Sumatran Tiger and its habitat.

Get Our FREE Books Now!

kidsonearth.life

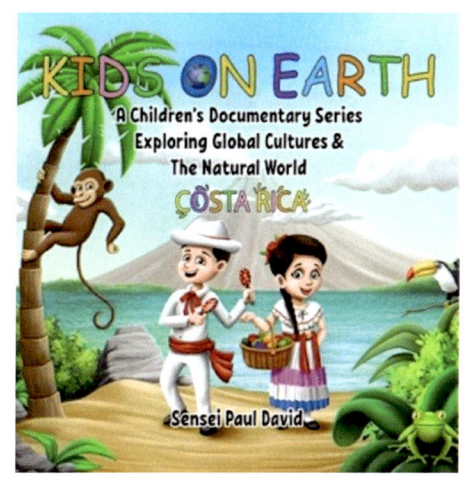

kidsonearth.world

Click Below for Another Book In Each Series

senseipublishing.com/KoE_SERIES

senseipublishing.com/KoE_Wildlife_SERIES

KoE En Español

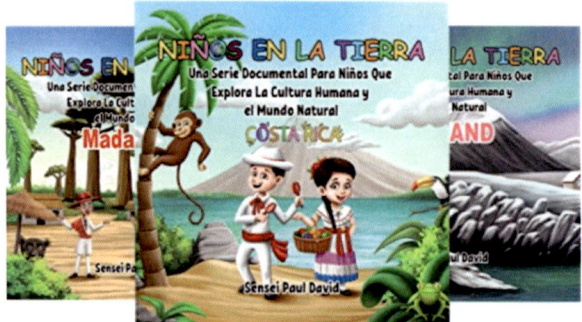

senseipublishing.com/KoE_SERIES_SPANISH

www.senseipublishing.com

Join Our Publishing Journey!

If you would like to receive FUTURE FREE BOOKS and get to know us better, please click www.senseipublishing.com and join our newsletter by entering your email address in the pop-up box.

Follow Our Blog: senseipauldavid.ca

Follow/Like/Subscribe: Facebook, Instagram, YouTube: @senseipublishing

Scan the QR Code with your phone or tablet to follow us on social media:

Like / Subscribe / Follow

Introduction

Welcome to the world of the Sumatran Tiger! This unique and fascinating creature lives in the jungles of Indonesia and is the only tiger species found exclusively in the country. This book will provide you with 30 fun and unique facts about the Sumatran Tiger that you won't find anywhere else. From the tiger's looks and behavior, to its habitat and diet, this book will teach you all about this incredible species and its place in the Indonesian rainforest. So let's get started and explore the world of the Sumatran Tiger!

The Sumatran Tiger is the smallest of all the living tiger species.

The Sumatran Tiger has the deepest and loudest roar of any living tiger species.

The Sumatran Tiger has a unique stripe and fur pattern.

The Sumatran Tiger is an endangered species with an estimated population of only around 400 individuals.

The Sumatran Tiger is an apex predator and has no natural predators in the wild.

The Sumatran Tiger is an ambush predator and relies on its camouflage to sneak up on its prey.

The Sumatran Tiger is an expert hunter and has been known to take down prey much larger than itself.

The Sumatran Tiger is an excellent swimmer and can often be found swimming in rivers and streams.

The Sumatran Tiger is an excellent climber and can often be found in trees.

The Sumatran Tiger can run up to speeds of 50 mph.

The Sumatran Tiger is a solitary creature and usually only comes together for mating purposes.

The Sumatran Tiger usually lives alone, but sometimes forms small groups of up to four individuals.

The Sumatran Tiger is an excellent tree climber and can often be found sleeping in trees.

The Sumatran Tiger is a nocturnal hunter and is most active at night.

The Sumatran Tiger is an expert tracker and can follow a scent for miles.

The Sumatran Tiger is an excellent swimmer and can hold its breath for up to 4 minutes.

The Sumatran Tiger is an excellent fisher and can often be found fishing in rivers and streams.

The Sumatran Tiger is an expert jumper and can jump up to 12 feet in the air.

The Sumatran Tiger has an impressive roar and can be heard up to 5 miles away.

The Sumatran Tiger is a powerful hunter and can take down prey up to three times its size.

The Sumatran Tiger is a solitary creature and prefers to hunt alone.

The Sumatran Tiger is a solitary creature and prefers to mate alone.

The Sumatran Tiger is an excellent tree climber and can often be found sleeping in trees.

The Sumatran Tiger is an expert escape artist and can often be found climbing over fences and walls.

The Sumatran Tiger has a keen sense of smell and can often be found sniffing out prey.

The Sumatran Tiger is an expert swimmer and can often be found hunting in rivers and streams.

The Sumatran Tiger is a powerful hunter and can take down prey up to three times its size.

The Sumatran Tiger is an expert tracker and can follow a scent for miles.

The Sumatran Tiger is a solitary creature and prefers to hunt alone.

The Sumatran Tiger is an endangered species and is facing the threat of extinction due to habitat destruction and poaching.

Conclusion

The Sumatran Tiger is a unique and fascinating species that is found only in Indonesia. This book provided you with 30 fun and unique facts about the Sumatran Tiger that you won't find anywhere else. From the tiger's looks and behavior, to its habitat and diet, this book has taught you all about this incredible species and its place in the Indonesian rainforest. We hope you enjoyed learning about the Sumatran Tiger and that you will help to protect and preserve this species for generations to come.

Thank you for reading this book!

If you found this book helpful, I would be grateful if you would **post an honest review on Amazon** so this book can reach other supportive readers like you!

All you need to do is digitally flip to the back and leave your review. Or visit amazon.com/author/senseipauldavid click the correct book cover and click on the blue link next to the yellow stars that say, "customer reviews."

As always…

It's a great day to be alive!

Share Our FREE eBooks Now!

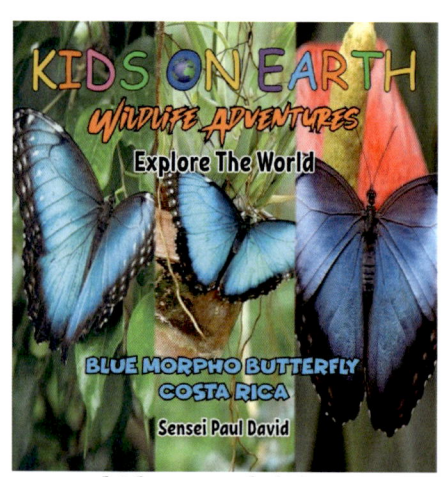

kidsonearth.life

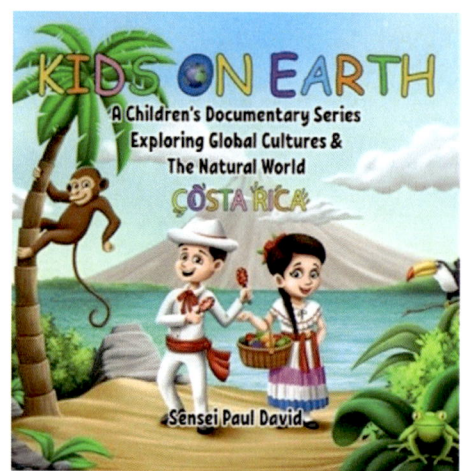

kidsonearth.world

Click Below for Another Book In Each Series

senseipublishing.com/KoE_SERIES

senseipublishing.com/KoE_Wildlife_SERIES

KoE En Español

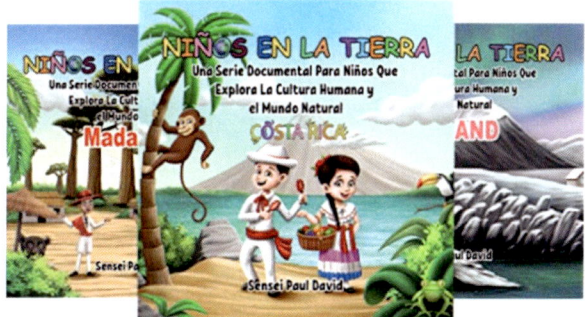

senseipublishing.com/KoE_SERIES_SPANISH

www.senseipublishing.com

www.senseipublishing.com

@senseipublishing
#senseipublishing

Check out our **recommendations** for other books for adults & kids plus other great resources by visiting
www.senseipublishing.com/resources/

Join Our Publishing Journey!

If you would like to receive FREE BOOKS and special offers, please visit www.senseipublishing.com and join our newsletter by entering your email address in the pop-up box

Follow Our Engaging Blog NOW!
senseipauldavid.ca

Get Our FREE Books Today!

Click & Share the Links Below

FREE Kids Books
lifeofbailey.senseipublishing.com
kidsonearth.senseipublishing.com

FREE Self-Development Book

senseiselfdevelopment.senseipublishing.com

FREE BONUS!!!
Experience Over 25 FREE Engaging Guided Meditations!

Prized Skills & Practices for Adults & Kids. Help Restore Deep Sleep, Lower Stress, Improve Posture, Navigate Uncertainty & More.

Download the Free Insight Timer App and click the link below:
<u>http://insig.ht/sensei_paul</u>

About Sensei Publishing

Sensei Publishing commits itself to helping people of all ages transform into better versions of themselves by providing high-quality and research-based self-development books with an emphasis on mental health and guided meditations. Sensei Publishing offers well-written e-books, audiobooks, paperbacks, and online courses that simplify complicated but practical topics in line with its mission to inspire people toward positive transformation.

It's a great day to be alive!

About the Author

I create simple & transformative eBooks & Guided Meditations for Adults & Children proven to help navigate uncertainty, solve niche problems & bring families closer together.

I'm a former finance project manager, private pilot, jiu-jitsu instructor, musician & former University of Toronto Fitness Trainer. I prefer a science-based approach to focus on these & other areas in my life to stay humble & hungry to evolve. I hope you enjoy my work and I'd love to hear your feedback.

- It's a great day to be alive!
Sensei Paul David

Scan & Follow/Like/Subscribe: Facebook, Instagram, YouTube: @senseipublishing

Scan using your phone/iPad camera for Social Media
Visit us at www.senseipublishing.com and sign up for our newsletter to learn more about our exciting books and to experience our FREE Guided Meditations for Kids & Adults.

www.ingramcontent.com/pod-product-compliance
Lightning Source LLC
Chambersburg PA
CBRC090902080526
44587CB00008B/173